Dating rEvolution

Or how to date like a man and get away with it

Rachael Zavala

With Contributions by Brion Porter
Cover Art by Colin Adams

Please see our web site at http://www.phmoms.com

Printed in the United States of America

Cover design by Colin Adams

Published by CreateSpace

ISBN-10: 1-4348-2794-1
ISBN-13: 978-1-4348-2794-4

Dedicated to "The Girls,"
my three beautiful children,
Michael, Sara and Sammy,
my loving partner, Brion,
and the best ex-husband in the whole world, Dave.

Contents

Preface

My name is Rachael Zavala and I am not a psychologist or doctor. I am just a regular chick who had an enormous amount of fun out in the real dating world. I wrote this book hoping this compilation of stories and suggestions will help other regular chicks enjoy dating as much as I did....

My mother was single in the post birth-control landscape of the 1980s. The dating scene for a single mother was abysmal and cheerless, with an inordinate amount of time wasted on spectacularly dysfunctional relationships. A teenager at the time, I wondered why anyone would engage in this pointless endeavor when she could have been doing almost anything else (like a hot poker to the eye) and having more fun.

I found myself single after an eleven-year marriage and the birth of three beautiful children. With vivid memories of my mother's single-mom experience, and a desire to avoid more of the same, I researched contemporary courting rituals, determined to do better. Hours were spent on my back porch with a glass of Château Potelle Chardonnay reading

The Rules, Why Men Love Bitches and many other fashionable books on love and relationships.

These books were entertaining and informative but something about their underlying hypotheses did not compute. Why did men hold all the cards? And why was it assumed men were either stupid or jerks? Why were women encouraged to manipulate a man into committing to them by dubious machination? It wasn't necessarily their methods that were suspect; it was the basic implications about men and women. This puzzling tidy bowl of questions swirled in my mind.

First of all, the vast majority of men are neither stupid OR jerks. Secondly, with the ink not dry on my divorce the last thing I wanted to do was jump into another relationship. Landing a man? No thank you! I just wanted quality (safe) sex.

I surmised my aversion to settling down made me exempt from elaborate mating rituals; since I didn't want a boyfriend/husband I didn't need to follow "The Rules." I dipped a toe in the dating world expecting lots of casual no-strings-attached sex with a plethora of commitment-phobic, hot men.

Then something unexpected happened. The men I wanted to date casually wanted to date me seriously. So much for the myth that all men are just looking for tawdry sex! I was a 30-something mother of three carrying 25 extra pounds and suddenly I was a hot dating commodity and giving my "I am not ready to be exclusive speech" every few weeks. It didn't make sense!

I started to ponder the dichotomy between those books and my experiences. Why was my dating experience so different? The men I was meeting were sweet and romantic, they certainly were not jerks. And, most shockingly, these men were very open to commitment. The crux of the matter was they wanted to find someone *they felt was right for them.*

So how was I, without any effort or intention on my part, becoming Ms. Right? I certainly wasn't playing elaborate mind games. I wasn't sitting in silence on early dates to appear more "mysterious" I wasn't avoiding their calls to show them how hard to get I was. I wasn't being a bitch.

I was living in the moment and enjoying myself with no elaborate agenda. I was making my safety and mental health the top priority at all times. I was being completely truthful. I was being myself.

By genuinely being my top priority, I was modeling the type of behavior I would accept from others. I was perfectly happy to live my life focusing on priorities like hobbies, education, kids and friends. My girlfriends teased me for dating like a man, but it was working!

Over the years I'd heard their stories of dating dreariness, so similar to my mom's experiences. By living for relationships and men instead of living for themselves, they diminished their quality of life. The contrast between my experiences and theirs led to an epiphany I shared with my circle of friends.

My Epiphany and our learning experiences led to a manifesto called "How to Have Sex Like a Man, and Get Away with It." Dating rEvolution is a compilation of the triumphs and failures of our subsequent revolution and evolution. We hope by sharing them you will skip the disheartening parts and go straight to the fun!

The Epiphany

If the Fates came to you and said, "In exactly five years time you will meet your soul mate and live happily ever after and there is no way to speed up or delay the process." How would you live your life differently right now? Would you go back to school or go backpacking across Europe? Would you spend more time on your current platonic relationships that are fulfilling and rewarding for you? How would you live your life differently if you were not focusing so much energy on dubious relationships?

I don't mean to imply that men are culturally or anthropologically more "evolved" than women. I am proposing the dating field is level for men and women for the first time since the dawn of human kind. Women have more independence and control than our great grandmothers could have dreamed was possible due to two significant changes that came about in the 1960s, birth control and women entering the work force *en mass* and demanding equal pay.

Until reliable and easily accessible birth control was available it was difficult for women to have the same freedoms and choices as our male counterparts. Women carry a child for nine months, while for some men the reproductive "work" can take as little as two or three minutes. Women were forced to be chaste or shoulder the burden of unwanted pregnancies. Combined with the inability to earn a living wage in pre-1960s America, it was downright irresponsible for women to have unprotected sex.

While women still face hurdles in the working world, the option to be self supporting is authentic for modern women. We have the expectation of gainful employment and the full spectrum of educational possibilities. We are no longer forced to "marry well" to live a comfortable life. This means we have an enormous amount of choice in to whom and when we get married (or not!).

Despite our modern reality, women everywhere are still living with the ghosts and obligations of the 1950s woman. Theoretically, we have modern adaptations that eliminate the need to be chaste or marry for security. Our freedom and choices should be limitless, yet we still live with the liability of the "the double standard" and other archaic social mores.

Like our appendix, pre-1950s puritanical social conditioning has no function in our modern world. If your appendix gets infected or otherwise harms your quality of life, it is surgically removed. If obsolete remnants of an iniquitous past are getting in the way of your happiness, they should be removed as well.

This is a collection of stories and examples (both good and bad) of a group of women who decided to jettison old fashioned ideals and look at dating from a fresh perspective and philosophy. This book is not for the faint of heart. The language is modern and frank. There are several chapters devoted to sex, its practice and consequences. This book will not appeal to, and nor is it written for, people who feel sex is an act that should be saved for the holy bonds of matrimony. I totally respect your choices, but this book is not going to speak to you.

The most common thing I heard while writing the book was something along the lines of, "People are not self aware and you have to be abnormally introspective and brave to (1) recognize and (2) reject intensive social conditioning." I was philosophizing that women have the same level of control and choice in their lives that men do but you would have thought I was suggesting people could fly if they just tried hard enough!

There is something disturbing about the presupposition that women are too clueless and weak to recognize and reject arcane canons that serve no purpose in their lives. This is absolutely not the case as I can counter that sentiment with a list of women who have easily and happily absorbed the philosophy with great personal success. In fact, it's sparked rEvolutions that continue to reverberate in positive ways with women all over the United States. Living an authentic life on your own terms is absolutely possible for all women and a good thing.

Think of this book as friendly guide, from one girlfriend to another, to inspire and make you laugh. It started as a series of notes, emails and blogs about dating, love, and the curious modern dichotomy of female independence and strength versus what is expected of "good girls" everywhere. Like the intellectual salons of the Victorian Era, philosophies were taken apart and put back together after deep examination (and much wine) and real life experimentation. The things that didn't "feel right" were rejected and changes were put into practice with varying degrees of failure and success. This book is our gift of love to you, from one woman to another. May you find inspiration in its pages.

I especially want to thank Misty, Rhonda, Laina and my many other friends who were willing to try something new and reaped the benefits. You ladies are inspirational on so many levels and your love and encouragement have meant the world to me. I also want to thank Brion, my lover and partner.

Chapter 1
Don't Settle!

There is a way that nature speaks, that land speaks.
Most of the time we are simply not patient enough,
quiet enough, to pay attention to the story.

~Linda Hogan

My friend Melanie* is magnificent; she is smart, funny and sexy. Melanie dated Sam for five years. Melanie stoically believed Sam was a "fixer-upper." Sam's abusive childhood was the excuse du jour for his myriad issues and inconsiderate behavior.

She grew up in a practicing Christian household and believed strongly in the institution of marriage and wanted children very much. He on the other hand, swore he would never get married and was justifiably afraid that his abusive past would make him a poor candidate for parenthood.

How did she end up settling for someone with vastly different life goals? Melanie was 30 pounds overweight and felt that he was the best she could do. She was willing to give

All names have been changed (except Eric's) to protect privacy.

up being a mother and wife, in addition to resigning herself to living with a man with serious psychological problems, because Sam was willing to date someone carrying a few extra pounds.

After many discussions, debates, desperate arguments and near break-ups over the marriage/kids issue, Sam got drunk one night and asked Melanie to marry him. It was a bitter-sweet and hollow victory.

When she told the rest of us at Thai food one Wednesday afternoon, we were horror-stricken. Our gorgeous and fabulous friend was about to make a horrible mistake. He wasn't a bad person for being honest with Melanie and she wasn't stupid or crazy for wanting marriage and family; they just wanted opposite things out of life. I felt bad for Sam and bad for Melanie.

Six months later Melanie was sitting on my couch the night before Thanksgiving. I'd invited a few friends over for holiday libation. One person noticed Melanie wasn't wearing her engagement ring and congratulated Melanie for coming to her senses; he'd heard from Sam they were not getting married. Sadly, Melanie hadn't heard about the broken engagement and had only taken the ring off to work on a project. Talk about an awkward moment!

Devastated, Melanie and Sam spent Thanksgiving discussing their needs and why he discussed his change of heart with his drinking buddies and not Melanie. After a teary and tense holiday, Melanie was finally fed up enough to walk away from the relationship. We all breathed a sigh of relief, but what in Thor's name took her so long to give up a situation that was so clearly unsuitable?

Was Sam really a jerk in this situation? Or was Melanie not listening to the message everyone else seemed to hear so clearly? Sam made it clear he was not interested in marriage and babies very early in their relationship. Five years had gone by while they had argued about an issue they had both been aware of from the day they met.

I met Melanie for Indian food and asked her why she had settled for such an irreconcilable and incompatible situation? I gave her the speech: **"What if the Fates had decided to send the perfect man for you in five years** and there was nothing you could do to speed up the process? How would you live your life differently? Would you keep wasting time and energy on the wrong guy or would you do something else?

What (horrors) if you were in a relationship with Mr. Wrong when Mr. Right showed up and then were too busy trying to make a crappy relationship work to notice him?

Have you thought about only dating casually and not getting attached to anyone unless they met your most stringent criteria? All the time you see guys shoot for the girl of their dreams and treat the rest like place markers. Why don't you do that?"

She started "dating like a man." Every day we would talk and she would say, "I can't believe how much fun this is!" She had more dates and interested men that she could schedule into a busy week! A lifetime of "I am not thin enough" to attract quality men went flying out the window. She was clearly being treated like a very desirable woman.

One of the biggest secrets of the dating world is we are doing men a FAVOR when we are selective. Men complain that we don't know what we want. We give mixed signals; they just can't figure us out! When women take the time to figure out what they want and then settle for nothing less we take the "crazy" out of the equation. The "Crazy" is when we settle for what we don't really want and then try to fake it, or worse try to force some poor man to change when we are not really sure what we want in the first place.

Now in a committed relationship with a spectacular man who shares important life aspirations for family and tradition and worships her like a goddess, she just shakes her head when she sees other women settle.

There is a joke that goes like this: A guy runs into his buddy at a bar and asks him, "What happened to your arms!?" The guy answers, "I woke up next to this ugly woman after drinking too much at the bar and had to chew my arm off to get out of there!" The friend says, "That explains one arm, what about the other?" The guy answers, "Well I chewed the other one off so I would never do it again!"

This joke would never be told with a woman as the protagonist because too many would spend the next five years miserably trying to polish that turd up! You can't date like a man if you force the OOOOOPS!-sex into a relationship.

One of the primary differences between men and women is men are aware that not every relationship is "the one" and they are ok with that. Casually dating a nice guy who isn't "the one" can be educational and a lot of fun, but you still have the choice to stay emotionally distant and wait for something better. Know what you want and settle for nothing less.

Knowing what you want also means knowing what you don't want. Some things are non-negotiable and every savvy woman should have a list of deal-breakers. If you date someone who has a deal-breaker issue that cannot be resolved, you are settling for less than what you need. Deal-breakers are individual to each person and you should be very aware yours. Here is a list of general deal-breakers. This is just the basics — many people have other more specific issues. For example, my friend Becca has a very strict hygiene requirement; she just can't date someone who is not fastidious about their cleanliness. *Feel free to add your own individual deal-breakers to the list!*

Married to someone else

There is no excuse to date a married man. You can get casual sex from a single guy just as easily and squander far fewer ethics.

Kids/no kids

Jacquie was a lovely lady who had been raised in the Mormon faith. She was twenty-seven when she met Tony who was divorced with three teenage boys. They fell passionately in love and she moved in a few months later. She adored his boys and broached the subject of children and how much she wanted a child of her own. He was stunned; not only did he have zero desire to have additional children; he had a vasectomy years before. They spent months trying to work out a way for her to fulfill a desire that had been culturally ingrained in her from birth, and still accommodate his needs.

Last I heard they had decided that she could get artificially inseminated and he would be the step-dad to the child. Would you be content with this compromise? Wanting or not wanting kids is a serious deal-breaker.

Marriage

You want marriage and he doesn't; the ever present dilemma. If he is telling you he never wants to get married, believe him. What he is saying is he never wants to get married to **you**. Too often a friend bemoans their man doesn't want to get married and a year later the guy is getting married to someone else.

Now, if you live in a hippie commune where free-love is the way of life and marriage is culturally verboten, then it's plausible marriage is not on the register. And if he's been through a divorce in the last two or three years, give the guy a break! He isn't ready to contemplate marriage yet. But otherwise, if you want marriage and he doesn't, it's not the right situation for you.

Drug/alcohol addiction

Drug and alcohol addiction, and/or smoking cigarettes can be deal breakers too if you don't share those habits. A friend from high school, Tanya, was married to Mike.

They were both heroine addicts and it really seemed to work out for them. When she got pregnant and decided to clean up, the problems started. Mike didn't want to be clean. Tanya didn't want to bring her baby into a world of drug addiction and was working hard to maintain her sobriety.

It took them five years, destroyed credit, and several visits by Child Protective Services before they could both get clean and stay clean together. Drug and alcohol addiction destroys lives; avoid potential partners who might have these issues.

Sexual incompatibility

My friend Gabriel met a beautiful young woman in Vegas and after a whirlwind courtship, they were married. I spoke to her briefly about what she did for fun and she mentioned bondage clubs. I was surprised since I had known Gabriel for years and he had never indicated he might be into BDSM.

Flash forward five years and Gabriel and his wife have an "open" relationship because they like very different things in bed. He is sleeping with porn stars in Vegas while she has a regular boyfriend she ties up and spanks, who she falls in love with and leaves him for. If there is a huge discrepancy in what turns you on, there is very little chance the relationship is going to be fulfilling over the long term.

Habitual lateness or inability to keep commitments

A man who is habitually late does not respect you. Especially with men, actions speak much louder than words. In fact, early on in a relationship, ignore anything that isn't backed up 100% by behavior and actions. When Brion and I started dating, there were several hopeful women waiting in the wings for him to give them their shot. One of them was a close friend of my roommate at the time. My roommate lamented her friend was getting stood up by "some guy" and was broken hearted. I finally figured out "some guy" was Brion.

The reason he was ignoring her calls was because he'd met me and had no time for other woman. His actions clearly defined what he wanted (to me and to her). Listen to what their actions are saying to you.

Chapter 2
Avoid the *Crazy*

Here's all you have to know about men and women: women are crazy, men are stupid. And the main reason women are crazy is that men are stupid.
~George Carlin

I disagree with Mr. Carlin that men are stupid. If I were to rewrite this quote it would read: "Women are crazy and men are clueless. They are inversely proportional; the more clueless the man, the crazier the women."

Once you are being crazy, it is very difficult to take a step back and reassess what is going wrong. So the best thing to do is *avoid the crazy all together.* This means assessing early and often how you feel. If you are feeling crappy or pathetic take a step back immediately! And if casual sex with strangers is turning you into an irrational psycho stalker, you probably shouldn't be having casual sex, regardless of whether you think you are "just like" Samantha from the popular HBO series *Sex and the City.*

What does "*crazy*" look like to a man?

• *Calling, text paging or emailing him frequently (any excuse is a good one to make contact with him).*

I was sitting at a bar with a friend. We'd met for drinks and were having an in depth conversation about how awesome it was for her to finally be single and having so much fun. She got a text page and switched off. For the next hour she was totally preoccupied with text paging her "friend with benefits." She ignored me, her food, and everything else. This was obviously not a casual relationship to her any more. The *crazy* was on its way!

• *Suddenly becoming good friends with a guy's mom/sister or the wife of his best friend, when no relationship existed before.* My friend Patty had been casually seeing a guy in her home town. He got spooked by her increasing demands and ended the relationship. She became his little sister's new "best friend" shortly after he bade her farewell. The little sister was thirteen years her junior and socially awkward. We (her friends) were stuck with this underage goober for six months while she clung to this tenuous tie to her previous f*ck buddy.[1] On a weekly basis she broke out the *crazy* as her friendship with the little sister afforded her the opportunity to see a veritable parade of his new f*ck-buddies and eventual fiancée.

- *Showing up "accidentally" at the guys favorite bar or hangout on a frequent basis.*

I got a frantic call from Samantha one night begging me to come to a new brew pub downtown. I was all cuddly in my pajamas but she wouldn't take no for an answer. She showed up at my door step, tossed me in the shower and offered to pay for my drinks and dinner. Finally, I acquiesced and we headed out. We walk into the bar and who do I see? Some guy she'd been seeing who had stopped calling her recently.

After kicking her under the table for dragging me out of my Jack Skellington pajamas for *this* disaster, I watched one of the more painfully awkward dating incidents ever. He sprinted around the room avoiding her. When she finally cornered him, all the while failing miserably at trying to appear like she wasn't stalking him, he humiliated her by loudly telling her to go away in the middle of a crowded urban bar.

- *Saying all you want is sex, and then sending them long loving emails about your family and what your dreams and aspirations are.*

There is simply no reason to contact a casual companion unless you are meeting up for something. My friend James is a ladies' man. In a polyamorous[2] relationship with a spectacular lady, he is unavailable for anything more than sex and friendship. The minute one of his casual partners starts sending emails that state anything more than a date and time for sex, he stops feeding the kitty[3]. He doesn't want to be added to the list of friends you send jokes to, or sweet notes about what you are doing that day.

If you are in a casual relationship and suddenly you are sending daily emails to a guy, you may be putting yourself on unsafe footing and could slip into some *crazy*.

- *He likes hockey so you suddenly acquire tickets to the game.*
Lisa was a workaholic. She met George on a business trip and they had a one night stand. She knew he had a girlfriend but it was the first decent sex she'd had in months

and he lived only 30 minutes away. He mentioned he was an avid San Jose Sharks fan (aren't we all!?) during the pre-sex conversation. She spent a few days staring at his contact information before sending him an email casually mentioning she had tickets to see the Sharks the following Saturday, and would he like to go?

Lisa became his frequent game buddy and occasionally slept with him even though she knew he had a girlfriend and was emotionally unavailable. *Crazy* came to live with Lisa for a year while she tried to pressure George into something more substantial than hockey games and sex. She still loves the Sharks, but she and George no longer speak.

• *Trying to monopolize his free time when you barely know each other.*

The girls and I went to PF Chang's for drinks and the local singles scene one brisk fall night. I was designated driver and Rebecca took full advantage by tossing back a few alcoholic beverages. She met Tom and went back to his place with him that night.

At a lunch date a few weeks later she expressed frustration with Tom's "flakiness." She'd called him the morning after they met to arrange another meeting but he'd been unwilling to commit to anything concrete saying that he was busy all week with a difficult deadline at work. She called him the following day to check again but his story hadn't changed; still busy at work. He met up with her one more time a week later for sex and then stopped returning calls.

I saw Tom months later at a local Starbucks and he joined me with his latte. He volunteered that he really liked Rebecca but he really was busy at work on a long term project with brutal deadlines. When it became clear that she would be unsympathetic to his priorities, he decided the relationship would be detrimental. While he liked her, he did not have a substantial enough investment in the relationship to overcome initial concerns.

• *A guy dumps you and you decide to move 600 miles to his hometown and try to pawn the move off as a good idea because "there are good jobs there."*

My gorgeous friend Heather graduated college with a prestigious post-graduate degree and spent that summer flying back and forth on the weekends to sleep with a nice guy who was in the middle of a divorce. She started pushing for a more serious relationship and he bolted; still reeling from his divorce he was unable to give her what she wanted.

Instead of doing the sane thing and getting on with her life, she started looking for work 600 miles away, in the same town as the guy who just dumped her! Her friends were aghast, and told her she was on a speeding locomotive headed towards Stalker-ville, but she insisted that there was "a lot of work in his town." As if there were no other place in the whole world she could get work with her very prestigious degree.

This convinced nobody, not us and certainly not the guy. She hasn't moved yet, but I suspect that once she moves to a new town where she knows few people and he is engaging in a post-divorce porn-star sex frenzy and still uninterested in dating Heather, the *crazy* will give her a giant spanking.

- *Any kind of damaging of personal property.*

In her hit song, "Before He Cheats," Carrie Underwood teaches her cheating boyfriend a lesson by destroying his truck with a baseball bat. Destroying personal property is not only illegal — it's BAT-SHIT *CRAZY*. If I were Carrie, I would invite over three of the hottest horniest guys I knew to pack his crap up into a PODS (to be left on the lawn) and then go out and party my butt off with my girls.

> *Insanity is often the logic of an accurate mind overtasked.*
>
> *~Oliver Wendell Holmes Sr*

Now that we've established what the *crazy* looks like, let's talk about how we get there. One of my favorite dating books, *Be Honest--You're Not That Into Him Either: Raise Your Standards and Reach for the Love You Deserve* by Ian Kerner states (paraphrased) that 65% of the time when a man puts his penis into a woman, she will start planning the wedding and naming the babies. I would guess that ratio to be closer to 80%. I call this the "80% Rule." (Men, by the way, do NOT do this. They are generally happy to be getting laid.)

The most vulnerable time for a woman to start acting crazy (taking the slow train to Patheticland as we like to call it) is right after sex with someone new and the 80% Rule kicks in. All of a sudden we are secretly wondering if that villa in Spain is still available for private weddings.

Waking up in our make-up with a hang-over and a brand new agenda that we have precariously little control over is never the best way to start the day. Unexpectedly we have turned into hopelessly addicted gamblers going "all in" with the most important parts of ourselves; betting everything recklessly that Mr. Last Night will call us in a timely manner and validate our worthiness and lovability. A man would never do this, and for good reason!

Do you think when you don't call a guy he is sitting around pouting? Do you think he's pining away wondering if he is "the one." More likely he's got a stogie in his mouth, a beer in his hand and he's playing poker with the guys. And doesn't that sound like more fun?

If you are calling a guy, or posting to his Myspace[4] every day, or sending long emails you are taking the first baby steps to the *crazy*. Just because he's slept with you does not mean you now have a binding contract making him responsible for your happiness and self worth. Realize that you only have control over your own reactions, behavior and agenda.

The second most precarious point is about six weeks after the sex and things seems to be moving along nicely. You've met his friends, you are his usual Saturday night date, he calls regularly and you are on your way to a more serious relationship. Finally, you both drop your guard and meet the real person behind the idealized representative that's been marketed thus far. You see each other for the first time without the fog of new-sex distracting you from harsh reality.

This can be a time when some women start losing themselves in a relationship and forego their regularly scheduled routine to make room for a boyfriend. As they get increasingly dependent on their new man for entertainment and attention and demands increase, it is likely he will take some time to reassess whether he is willing and able to fulfill these demands. After examining the scale with the good and easy things on one side (sex any time, you get along great) and his required output (Are you getting too clingy? does he really want to spend every holiday with your crazy parents?), he will determine whether they balance in his favor. Getting clingy at this juncture is nearly always a death knell for even a promising relationship.

This is a great time for a confident woman to take a step back. Get back in touch with all of the things that gave you pleasure before you started dating Mr. Wonderful. Too often the natural lull between lust at first site and a deeper more meaningful relationship is right around the six week mark. It makes us women *crazy*.

In summary, the two most hazardous times when a woman might get on the slow train to Pathetictown is after sex with someone new and also six weeks after the first sex. Don't get on that train! Beware these times and do everything you can to maintain your equilibrium and go about your normal business. Don't get crazy and don't get clingy!

Avoidance Tools

Now that we know what it looks like, and its prime cause (sex) how do we avoid the *crazy*? *Ideally,* you shouldn't be betting more than you are willing to lose in any sexual transaction because you would never gamble recklessly with something as important as your emotions. Alas this is not always realistic.

If you see yourself exhibiting any of the behaviors bullet pointed in this chapter the **only** thing you can do is get off the slow train to Patheticland at the next possible stop! Remove yourself from the situation and give yourself time to regain your bearings.

Focus on the enjoyable things in your life that you do have control over by making a list of fun things you love to do (see the *Conclusion* for a list of new hobbies and activities you might consider). Or even a list of things you don't mind doing too much. Anything is better than arriving depleted and depressed in Patheticland!

My Fun List

Or Things I'd Rather Do than Deal with Dating Drama

1. Sit on my back porch all snuggled up with a good book and watch the kids play in the sprinklers.

2. Take the kids to Santa Cruz Beach Boardwalk, lay out a big blanket and spend the day enjoying the rides and the ocean. Treat everyone to corn dogs and ice cream.

3. Sit in my 50 gallon jet tub with my new *Gourmet Magazine* and a nice bottle of Gamay Rouge until I am all pruney.

4. Go hang out at the pool with my friend, Victoria.

5. Take my little boat out on the Stockton Delta with a cooler stocked full of great food and icy beverages. Find a nice little beach and let the kids frolic in the water.

6. Hang out with Robin and Kelly at my summer place on the Delta and ingeniously cook grandiose meals in my tiny little kitchen by being crafty and using fancy pants cooking apparatus like an electric panini skillet or pizzelle maker.

7. Sew and weave, practice calligraphy.

8. Get a pedicure with Melanie and then hit Chipotle for a carnitas and corn salsa burrito.

9. Play all night topless dominoes with my girlfriends.

Even the coolest chick can get crazy when her mind is working over-time on an "all-in" wager that is about to go in the crapper. Never gamble with more than you are *willing to lose* because that is the only thing you have any control over. Make you own list (or borrow mine) of things you like to do and keep it handy for when you feel dating drama creep up on you. Most guys will go to great lengths to avoid being needy or neurotic *because being needy and neurotic sucks ass.*

Chapter 3
Know Your Limitations

*One's first step in wisdom is to question every-
thing – and one's last is to come to terms with
everything.* ~Georg C. Lichtenberg

O ne of the best ways to avoid the *crazy* is to seriously
and thoughtfully consider your personal limitations.
Not everyone can date causally, or have casual sex without
losing control. Knowing your limitations is harder than you
think! We all have a tendency to overestimate how calm,
cool and collected we are.

My friend Cara believed herself to be a real "player." She
would assure her f*ck-buddies that she only wanted free and
casual sex and would not get attached emotionally (and
earnestly begged them not to get attached to her). After two
or three dates, she was hooked and worse still... wouldn't
admit it!

She would text page her f*ck-buddy 10 times a day and
drop plans with her girlfriends at the last minute so she
could meet up with him. She would say, "I am not

emotionally invested, I just want sex!" We would go out and she would say, "There are no good single guys" and ignore the nice men trying to get her attention. She started hiding how often she was contacting him. Her actions did not match her words.

Inevitably chaos would ensue when her f*ck-buddy wasn't treating her like a GIRLFRIEND. In larger social gatherings she would loudly corner Mr. Casual and try to pin him down on "us"... you know the "us" that wasn't supposed to happen because they had clearly agreed to be just f*ck-buddies.

> Fictitious Hollywood examples of the modern single woman, like Samantha from the popular HBO series Sex in the City, model sexual confidence and detachment that is not generally realistic. A real woman's ability to maintain the same level of indifference is possible, but not likely.

Gradually she would work up to weeks of whining and complaining about the horrible jerk that treated her like a rube. The guy would be ostracized by our peers and the whole time I would just shake my head. It was pretty unfair to the poor man. She was not honest with herself or her lovers about what she wanted or was capable of and they had merely made the mistake of believing her cocky bravado.

In my personal experience, my limitation is two or three encounters. My friends would marvel at my ability to stay detached. I felt like a calm cool illusionist. Truthfully, I am like any other girl (We are hard-wired for bonding! Don't try to fight biology!). The difference is I know my limitations.

If I am not interested in more than a casual relationship with a man, I don't see him more than two or three times. Before you start having casual sex or casually dating, it is essential to figure out what your limitations are. Sadly, this is almost impossible to predict until you throw yourself into the dating world, but you can glean clues from what you know about yourself:

• Do you have a strong religious background that precludes having guilt free casual sex?

• Do you fall in love easily?

• Do you have self-esteem issues that will make you feel unlovable if someone you are dating casually can keep their emotional distance after having sex with you?

All casual sex has the potential for drama if people are not honest about what they want and need out of the situation. Don't take this lightly! The preservation of your mental state of mind and self esteem should always be your first consideration.

Chapter 4
Listen to Your Instincts!

One is not born a woman, one becomes one.
~Simone de Beauvoir,
The Second Sex

The hardest thing about dating like a man is to figure out what your personal boundaries and limitations are. There is no way to figure this out without some soul searching and trial and error. Most women are not Samantha from *Sex in the City*, wantonly able to bed multiple men without much in the way of attachment or anxiety. At the same time, most of us are not so needy that we instantly fall in love with every guy that comes down the pike. Most of us are somewhere in the middle.

So how do you figure out your limitations in a careful and responsible way? Get in touch with your inner voice and instincts! Far too often, women ignore that icky feeling in their stomach that something isn't right. Feeling anxious and insecure? The knot in your stomach is your soul's way of telling you something is not right. Listen!

The instant you get an icky feeling in a dating situation, it's time to politely excuse yourself and take your own sweet time to think about what your instincts are trying to tell you. Call your best friend, write in your diary, and/or chant your mantra. Do whatever you need to do to get familiar with your instincts and work consciously in conjunction with them.

> **The Man's perspective**
> By Brion Porter
> "In general, I don't treat women any different on a day-to-day/on-the-surface basis, regardless of what type of relationship we have. But what changes when I am in a committed relationship are the deeper interactions. I share more with my partner, trust her to a higher level... and here is the kicker, she is my priority in life."

When Melanie was in her dating phase she met a man that she had amazing chemistry with. He pursued her ardently with phone calls and emails. But there were things amiss; he was frequently flakey about their meetings and had a mysterious ex-wife lurking in the background.

Even though Melanie liked this man and could have easily fallen for him, she listened to her instincts early on and decided that she was too fabulous to waste a lot of emotional energy on a flakey guy. "Flakey" was not on her criteria list for the perfect man. Clean cup, move down.

Everyone can occasionally be late or forget to call and since you are tremendously busy having fun, you hardly notice. However, if a man is frequently dismissive of your time early on, throw that fish back. Keep on dating casually and looking for something better. If you are "the one," he will treat you like you are the most precious thing in the world. If he is treating you poorly or dismissively and you allow that behavior, you are doing yourself and everyone else a disfavor.

In conclusion, when you listen to your instincts and understand what your needs are, everyone wins! Even if you just pause for sixty seconds to evaluate what your gut is saying, you will be more in control of what is happening to you and around you! Self awareness is a beautiful thing.

Chapter 5
Be Honest

Nothing is easier than self-deceit.
For what each man wishes, that he
also believes to be true.

~Demosthenes

It is far too common for women who have been in an unhealthy dating cycle to decide "The Rules" are right and sacrificing their integrity to the evil God/dess of the Ticking Biological Clock is a good idea. Bartering honor and honesty to "land the perfect man" has become the norm.

This has led men to *expect* dishonesty on a grand scale. Duplicitous messages like "Not calling means I like you... saying I don't want a relationship means I do... I am waiting six weeks before I will have sex with you" and so on are all part of the common dating landscape of our times.

Let me tell you why this is a bad idea (beyond the obvious). When we lie about fundamental aspects of ourselves, we sell ourselves short. You are totally fabulous and you know it! You don't need to be anything but yourself.

Plus, *all of this assumed dishonesty is making it difficult for those who don't use similar tactics.* It's like dating **de**volution!

My good friend Becca was closing out an unhealthy and repressive relationship when she met the dashing and well-read doctor. She made it clear that she was still recovering from some pretty intense damage and was interested in a strictly casual relationship. Since marrying a doctor is every mother's wet dream for their daughter and they had great chemistry, he didn't believe her.

Ironically, he assumed she was using "The Rules" on him and was scheming to land him. About four weeks into their friendship, she was surprised by a phone conversation full of angst and recrimination. He was angry at her for not being in love with him and dumbfounded that he had misread her "obvious" cues!

What had Becca done wrong? She treated him with kindness and respect, but definitely had her own life. She was busy and clearly not interested in an exclusive relationship, which she had explained to him honestly and unmistakably.

When she called me she was incredulous. Me, "DUH! Of course he thought you were using 'The Rules'! Don't hold it against him; you can't blame him for being madly in love with a confident hottie like yourself."

The Man's Perspective
By Brion Porter

You have to be careful about being completely honest about what you want. Women who have either purposefully or accidentally blurred or crossed this line quickly became "that girl I used to sleep with." And maybe not so surprising, these are the ones that come off as "clingers," which I am sure is the next step towards being a stalker. This brings me to ... Trust your instincts. If you feel your alarm bells going off for some reason, GET OUT! We all have a pretty good internal indicator about those potential partners that are either well suited or not to our desires and needs. In the end, being honest about what you want from a partner, casual or serious, is the quickest way for both of you to get what you want from the relationship.

We both had to pause for a moment and consider: It is a sad day when it is broadly assumed that women generally lie about fundamental wants and needs to con men into committing to them. And we call men jerks because they respond poorly to this emotionally unethical behavior?

No one wants to be lied to on a deep emotional level.

Chapter 6
Don't Be a "Clingon"

Bart! Stop pestering Satan!
~Marge Simpson

I cannot emphasize this enough, do not be a Clingon[5]! The most important tool for preventing the *crazy* is to forgo clingy behavior at all times. This is particularly important after sex for the first time with someone new.

We all know what a Clingon is. She is the girl that calls, text pages, and badgers. She follows some poor schmoe around the party with that wistful puppy dog look in her eyes. Long emails about her life and family are sent on a regular basis and attempts to secure as many minutes of his spare time border on harassment. He can drop by her place at all hours for "the booty call" and be assured of sex.

How did this unfortunate soul get there? How do we all

avoid going down that path? Once gain, by recognizing warning signs early and ceasing the behavior.

Signpost number one (previously addressed in Chapter 2 "Avoid the *Crazy*") is frequent calling/emailing/text-paging. Why should we avoid calling men? That seems like "game-playing"! The difference is I could care less how HE thinks about me calling or not calling, I only care about how it makes ME feel.

Very early in my dating experience I called a man I was seeing, he was at work and busy and distracted. It made me feel like I was not a priority and frankly, kind of crappy. When I get that crappy feeling, I take the time to pause and ask myself some hard questions. Why was I feeling bad? Was it because I felt like I was being impolite by calling him at work or when he might be busy? My feelings were hurt when it seemed like I was a nuisance. I decided I didn't like feeling like I was bothering him and wouldn't bother him any more.

When I waited for him to call me, he had time to talk and focus on our conversation. He wasn't in the middle of a client meeting or rush order and suddenly put on the spot to entertain me. He easily and painlessly got into a regular routine of setting aside time each day to talk to me.

> If he does not call you, he isn't interested in you. Trust me on this *If a guy wants to talk to you, he will figure out how to get in touch with you.* If he doesn't want to talk to you, as the Mad Hatter said, "Clean cup, move down!"

Boy, was that an easy lesson to learn! I don't have to lift a finger and a guy will call me when he is happy, not distracted and totally riveted by my every word? As a bonus I am never "that girl" who won't stop calling and bugging him at inopportune moments. And no more cycle of, "Why was he so abrupt with me? Is he giving me the brush off?" Everyone wins!

This is one way guys are ahead of the curve. They understand and expect occasional rejection. Be cocky like a man and say, "Their loss! I am spectacular! NEXT!"

> *No one can make you feel inferior without your consent.*
> *~Eleanor Roosevelt*

Another signpost is having sex without knowing your boundaries intimately (pardon the pun). I had a friend who drank too much at a party and went home with a guy she'd just met. She was newly single and recklessly decided to experiment with casual sex without putting any forethought into her wants, needs and personal boundaries.

In the end, it didn't matter to her they had nothing in common. It didn't matter that he was in a quasi-relationship with someone else and had five kids with different women. It didn't matter that he was "underemployed" and addicted to online porn. After they had sex the 80% Rule kicked in and she was taking the slow train to Patheticland. Never try to force a one night stand into something it's not because the 80% Rule has kicked in! (If you do this, you should probably forgo one-night stands until you are more comfortable with your personal limitations).

If by chance you find yourself in a horrible situation that makes you feel or act crazy, do anything you can to distance yourself from irrational behavior. Even if you can't stop the irrational feelings of attachment to Mr. Wrong, you CAN control your own actions. Treat your best friend to a trip to Vegas. Write the next great novel. Go sit in your jet tub for two days and read the new Harry Potter book with a magnum of wine and a basket of strawberries and chocolate. The five pounds you might gain will be easier to lose than the 170 pounds of dead weight you will gain dating Mr. Wrong.

Chapter 7
The Sex

If I am not having fun, it's not happening!
~Rachael Zavala

Sherry was freshly out of college when I met her. Drop-dead gorgeous with a body like a porn star (only with natural boobs), she was in a frustrating relationship with a young man who did not share her high sex drive. She was giving a lot of oral sex without much in the way of reciprocation.

As her duly appointed MILF, I was appalled and suggested there was something wrong with this picture. She assured me that she really enjoyed giving oral sex and didn't mind if that was all that happened. I asked, "What is his incentive to fulfill your needs if he is getting oral sex all the time without giving anything in return?" Four months later, the relationship ended in a blaze of crazy glory.

Every guy wants to be a good lover. Help them realize

their quest to be fabulous in bed by showing them what works for you. My boyfriend thinks it ROCKS that I am a selfish lover! He never has to worry that I am faking it.

> *How do I know I am good in bed?*
> *I come every time!*
> *~My Friend Eric*

To date like a man, you should be having orgasms every time or nearly every time; no guy on the planet would perform oral sex on you and not expect you to do something for him. They may have to put in overtime the first few times to get you to climax, but practice makes perfect! And what would you rather be doing on a Saturday afternoon anyway?

Let's be honest, not everyone can easily have orgasms vaginally. If you have to stimulate yourself manually, or he needs to perform oral sex for you, or however works best for you... that is exactly what should be happening!

Myth: There is such a thing as universally good in bed.

Why is this a myth? Because the most important part of good sex is compatibility and chemistry. I had a friend once who assured me that she gave the "best blow jobs" (I wondered how she knew? Did she win a blue ribbon at the fair?). I was so impressed I asked her for pointers and then double checked their veracity with my good friend Ray, who happens to be gay and knows something about giving and getting a blow job. He confirmed what I suspected; that might work for some guys, but not for his husband.

There are just too many complicated factors that come into play when it comes to sex and what a particular individual will enjoy. The movie *Secretary* starring Maggie Gyllenhaal is a perfect celluloid example of "someone for everyone." Her lover wanted to spank someone and she wanted to be spanked; the definition of a compatible lover.

I dated this guy once who had a fetish for blue fuzzy toilet seat covers. He'd done some sexual exploring at a very young age while sitting on a blue fuzzy toilet seat cover and as an adult needed to be rubbing the cover to orgasm. He kept them under his bed.

I spent weeks getting to know him before any hanky panky and was already emotionally invested before finding out he had a sexual quirk that was never going to work for me. It took me months to extract myself. I hope he found someone who has the same fetish because otherwise he was a great guy!

Being sexually compatible is not something that can be learned or faked. It has to do with your history, personality, life experiences and a million other things, not the least of which is chemistry. No one wants to find their mate is into cross dressing or BDSM if that isn't what they like.

Every time I hear from a girlfriend, "Sex is overrated!" I think to myself, what is wrong with this picture? Do they have compatibility issues with their partner? Do they feel guilty about enjoying sex due to societal pressure to be a "good girl"? Are they so nervous about their expectations they cannot put them aside long enough to enjoy sex?

Sex is generally considered to be an enjoyable thing. If it isn't for you, take some time to think about why and see if improvements can be made to enhance your experience. Once again, this type of exploring isn't the worst way you could spend a Saturday afternoon.

Additionally, on the off chance you don't know what an orgasm is, or have never had one, it is time to get down there and figure it out! They are awesome and everyone who is sexually active should be having them.

'Nuff said on that one.

Chapter 8
The Sex Part Deux

I used to be Snow White, but I drifted.

~ *Mae West*

Wikipedia defines "slut" as:"...a pejorative term for a person (usually female) who is deemed sexually promiscuous. The term has traditionally been applied to women and is generally used as an insult or offensive term of disparagement."

Like our appendix, the double standard is still around even though it no longer has a function. Before birth control became readily available it was disastrous for women to have sex with multiple partners. Women were far less likely to have access to gainful employment or child care and marrying the right man was an imperative to living a comfortable life. This is no longer the case.

It is unfortunate society continues to be conflicted about sexually confident women and conditions us from an early age to fear being labeled as promiscuous. Choose to put an and to the double standard by making your peace with the word "slut" and looking with disdain upon people who use pejorative statements to oppress a woman's sexuality.

It is total hooey that sex too soon ruins a relationship. How you act afterwards is much more important and can mess things up, but being quick to jump in the sack is not a cause for the ruination of a possible good thing. Being needy or clingy is a much more likely cause.

Do men flinch when someone calls them a "slut"? No, It's kind of a compliment; denoting their prowess and success with women. Being a sexual creature should not make you feel bad or "easy," and if it negatively impacts a new relationship that guy wasn't "the one" for you.

I met Brion at a rocking party I was throwing for friends. One of his ex-girlfriends introduced us at the end of the evening just as my hostess duties were wrapping up. Drop dead gorgeous in leather pants; he was a legendary ladies man within my peer group. After Allie introduced us he went to kiss my hand but "missed," kissed me on the lips and 20 minutes later we were naked. Two years later he is still completely devoted to me.

After I woke up (with a hang over) the morning after meeting Brion, I had party aftermath to clean up before leaving for a six hour car ride. I was anxious to get on with my day. His anxiety over my abrupt departure was adorable, but I didn't linger, I went and got my work done.

He gave me his contact info (I was preoccupied and forgot to give him mine). I never call guys because it makes me uncomfortable and I have found it to be unnecessary. Unfortunately, I had not gotten a chance to give him my contact info. He'd expressed very clearly that he wanted to see me again, in fact tracking down the only scrap of paper he could find (a post-it note) and writing a surprisingly lengthy two-sided note articulating this.

Finally able to relax and recap my weekend on the way back home, I asked my friend Aline what the current philosophy was on calling a guy. Was I supposed to wait a week or what? We decided I should probably wait three days, just to be safe. I emailed him the very next morning, to his delight.

But then the research began. Who was this guy? Was he worth going "all in"? He lived in Los Angeles and I lived in the San Francisco Bay Area. We shared many mutual friends who were honest with me about his wanton ladies-man reputation. There were some noteworthy obstacles that made me hesitate before placing a bet on a deeper relationship.

After doing my due diligence I came to the conclusion it would be best to avoid an exclusive relationship with someone with such a spotty record of monogamy, regardless of our obvious chemistry and compatibility. Even though I was attracted to him and we were compatible, I was still not willing to gamble my heart on a notorious womanizer. I suggested we try a polyamorous[1] relationship.

Then a peculiar thing happened, this man who had legions of women clamoring for his leather bedecked bottom insisted upon on monogamy. He firmly believed open relationships didn't last and he wanted ours to have a better chance of going the distance. And he sure as heck didn't want me sleeping with anyone else!

We opened "pre-datual negotiations," which was our

tongue-in-cheek way of talking casually about serious long term expectations. We sat down and openly discussed what our expectations were, what we wanted out of life and whether our plans meshed well enough to move forward together. He was committed to getting his job transferred to the Bay Area, which was our biggest obstacle. So we closed negotiations and agreed we were a couple.

Relationship books like "The Rules" clearly state if you have sex on a first date you are dooming the relationship to failure. The moral of my story is the sex is not the problem; it's how you act AFTER the sex. Becoming a clingy mess (or not) can make or break a relationship.

Not everyone is comfortable with sex before they really get to know someone. There are still ways you can get an idea of whether you might be sexually compatible. One way you can check out his sexual quirks without having sex with him first is to ask to see his porn.

I never date anyone until I see his masturbatory material even if I have to sneak a peek while he is at work. If he shows you porn that is all busty naturals from Sweden and you are flat chested and have dark hair, there are going to be problems down the road. If he refuses to show you his porn, his fetish is likely so vile, you don't want to know.

This is one of the few ways you can check out someone's quirks without sleeping with them. Albeit I have to admit my lovers find it either extremely funny or embarrassing when I want to see their porn... but it seems to always ends up pretty fun for both of us, if that is any consolation.

Obviously, if you have religious beliefs that strictly forbid pre-marital sex, you are going to have to roll the dice and see how it goes on your wedding night. I wish you well and totally respect your choice. But for all the non-virgins out there, if you have already had more than one partner, it's quibbling over semantics when it comes who is a "slut". You might as well just say screw-off to societal wording created to control a woman's sexuality and do what you want to do. Isn't that what Gloria Steinem and those fabulous ladies of the 60s and 70s took all that crap for, so we could create our own sexual destiny? Don't let them down!

Chapter 9
Consider the Future

> *I believe that we are solely responsible for our choices, and we have to accept the consequences of every deed, word, and thought throughout our lifetime.*
>
> ~*Elisabeth Kubler-Ross*

There are consequences for everything we do. With sex the consequences can be profoundly life altering and extremely serious. Pregnancy, sexually transmitted disease and emotional fall out are only some of the consequences that are possible with every sexual encounter. This is why "double bagging"[6] is your best bet.

Double bagging is the use of two birth control methods at all times. Double bagging is some type of permanent birth control, like an IUD or the pill in conjunction with condoms.

In a passionate moment a guy will occasionally try to talk a woman out of using a condom and then there is an awkward space in the conversation where you have to basically tell them you think they are probably diseased and won't have sex with them unless they cover their contaminated penis with a condom. This can kill the mood.

Generally, if a guy thinks you are capable of getting pregnant, they will not question the use of a condom. If a condom breaks, you will still have back-up protection from your IUD or the pill (or the shots or whatever) but it is absolutely necessary to use condoms in this day and age if you are sexually active to avoid getting STDs that can kill you. If you are too embarrassed to insist on a guy wearing a condom, this little white lie is the least of your worries.

Never tell a guy you are on birth control until you know how they feel about condom use. I know I am telling you to lie about being on birth control when I spent a lot of time telling you to be honest and you are probably a little disappointed in me. However this is just a little white lie and if you avoid pregnancy and AIDS I think it is well worth it!

Under no circumstances should anyone be sexually active and forgo condom use. Bring your own at all times. Don't leave this up to the guy. Your health and safety are the number one priority at all times. You don't care if he thinks you are a "slut" for having condoms because you reject pejorative statements that attempt to strip you of your control over your sexual destiny!

Chapter 10
Consider the Future Part Deux

Don't compromise yourself.
You are all you've got!
~Janis Joplin

O f special note, dating married (or "taken") men is universally a bad idea. There are great single men out there; it is up to you to set the standard that you will avoid married/taken men. The reasons for avoiding married men are threefold: massive potential for drama and self esteem loss; they are probably lying creeps and strong confident women do not sleep with men like that; and finally because you will lose face with your female friends who will recognize that you don't have enough self esteem to respect normal boundaries. Consider the future!

No woman, when she writes down the criteria for her perfect man, puts married in the pro column. It is not possible to set your standard lower than a man who (if he remains married) cannot meet your needs and if he leaves his wife, is probably going to cheat on you too. If "married" is anywhere on your criteria list, I would go down to your local adult hardware store, invest in a quality vibrator and avoid dating for a while. Chant the mantra, "I am fabulous and I deserve only the best" one thousand times each day.

The trade off for sleeping with married men is miniscule in comparison to the disastrous potential for damaging emotional fall out. Remember Glenn Close in Fatal Attraction? Deep inside we all knew that Michael Douglas was just asking for Ms. Psycho to ruin his life because he was a clueless guy and sleeping with her when he was married. Avoiding the *crazy* is nearly impossible when you start dabbling in married-man territory.

And don't give me this crap there are no single guys. I meet them all the time and I am a 30-something mother-of-three carrying 25 extra pounds. There are fabulous and wonderful single men out there and they are looking for quality (safe) sex. If they find love, that wouldn't be too bad either.

On a smaller scale, if you are casually dating, it is probably not a good idea to date within your close peer group if at all possible, even if they are single. It is too easy to turn Mr. Right Now into Mr. Right when you have to see him all the time. I know this seems contrary. You think to yourself wouldn't it be so convenient to share the same friends? But think about this, if you strictly date outside your peer group, if anything goes wrong, you automatically get to keep your friends!

Men want love as much as we do and will go to great lengths for someone they truly feel is right for them. They don't want to waste time or mislead a woman they know deep down is not "the one." Respect men enough to listen to what their behavior and words are telling you. Men value love and commitment enough to wait for the right thing. So should you!

Not to mention, you don't have to stress that once you break up he is jockeying for the friends by saying bad stuff about you (like telling everyone you have the worst PMS on the planet and are a slob). Besides, if he was so great, you wouldn't have waited until just NOW to start dating him. Don't poop where you sleep, if you know what I mean.

Chapter 11
Getting Out

Breaking up is hard to do.
~Neil Sedaka

B reaking up is hard to do, but it is even harder to do it with class! Maybe you've been reading this book and have come to the revelation that the man you are currently dating is not your soul mate and you would rather be free and clear for perfection, if it were to come along (good for you!). He could be a guy you've only been dating for a few weeks, or a guy you've been with for years. Either way, once you make the choice to put that fish back it's always best to try to be as classy as possible about it.

If he is part of your regular circle of friends this is especially important. People often have the desire to paint an ex-boyfriend/ex-husband in grotesque terms to justify a break up. This jockeying for support is very unfair to your friends and is totally unnecessary.

Sometimes things just don't work out, even between very good people.

There are many reasons a relationship goes bad. Often times it is a discrepancy in feeling or goals. Sometimes these two are intertwined. Whatever the reason for breaking up, keep in mind that you once cared about this person and when you are through the difficult aspects of relationship dissolution, friendship is always the best option if possible.

The first step to a classy break up is keeping things private. Of course, you are going to vent to your close friends about the things that went wrong, but do what you can to keep negative comments as close to your vest as possible. It makes you look like a cool, classy chick. Plus all of that whining and bad mouthing doesn't really make us feel better. It makes us feel petty and small. The sooner you can refocus on the good things in your life, the better!

If he chooses to air your dirty laundry, you have two choices. You can cling with both hands to the high ground and in a few weeks when the dust settles, every person you know will think you are awesome and he is a giant ass. Or you can get right down in the pig slop with him and you can both be asses. It is hard sometimes when we are hurting to keep that perspective, but have your Fun List handy and instead of throwing yourself head first into dating drama, you have Plan B for fun!

The best way to break up graciously is to point out to the guy that you think he is a great guy but you are looking for perfection and give him all the reasons (in a nice way) that neither of you are getting what you need from the relationship.

For example, after doing my due diligence on dating and reading all of those dating books, I went out into the dating world thinking that men were commitment averse and I could have my tawdry way with them without any danger they would try to wrangle me into a serious relationship. My first foray into casual dating quickly disproved this theory.

Jack was my neighbor at the resort where I kept my trailer and boat. He was 42 with gorgeous blue eyes and a great body. Single for the many years I'd known him, all of our neighbors whispered what a great guy he was and how odd he hadn't found someone special.

He seemed like a great candidate for a f*ck-buddy and I made my intentions known by slipping a condom in his pocket at a party I was catering. He thought it was hysterically funny and went from f*ck-buddy to boyfriend in the blink of an eye. After two weeks, he insisted he was not interested in a casual sex and we agreed to explore an exclusive committed relationship.

I made two rookie moves here. First, I dated someone unavoidable within my tight knit social circle; we actually owned real estate within a few steps of one another. Second, I did not make sure we were perfect for each other before going "all in." It was a case of attraction without sharing mutual life goals and we both quickly realized it. Now we were stuck with some unfortunate water under the bridge and our summer places were 20 yards from each other. It could have been a disaster!

I knew I needed to take a step back because I was feeling like a nut-job. I was sending him text pages twice a day and weekly emotive emails while I was tipsy. It was horrible, and when things feel horrible, I take a giant step back to study the situation. I knew I had to do some things differently.

I told him I was going to take some alone-time to ponder whether the differences in goals could be overcome. It seemed obvious to me that his once great passion for me had dwindled to an unacceptable level, primarily because we had glaring compatibility issues. So I broke up with Jack and decided to spend a week in Mexico on the cheap with the girls and then went camping with friends for a week to get my bearings. I came home refreshed and ready to move on.

Because of the awkwardness at the summer place, I avoided going there for a couple of months. It was important to give him his space. I also tried to avoid conversations with our mutual close friends about my broken heart. He made small gestures of kindness towards me that acknowledged the difficulty of our situation and expressed his desire to be friends. When I felt I was completely over him, I resumed hanging out with my friends and boating on a regular basis. We are still friends and he is a great neighbor and wonderful man.

I know it is hard to stay cool when you are feeling hurt and frustrated. It is still best to maintain your self respect, keep yourself sane and not pollute the waters where you spend your leisure time. Don't get crazy and don't get clingy.

If you are having trouble separating from a guy that you know is bad for you, I highly recommend you subject yourself to something Ian Kerner calls a "he-tox" in his book, *Be Honest — You're Not That Into Him Either: Raise Your Standards and Reach for the Love You Deserve.* A he-tox means quitting a guy cold turkey.

If it makes you sweat even thinking about a he-tox, then you need one! A bad relationship is like compulsive gambling. You keep placing bets addictively, even if it torpedoes your quality of life. You think to yourself, "Maybe this will change the tide and he'll start treating me better." Sadly, when emotional capital has been heavily invested, it can be difficult to cut your losses and walk away from the table.

Do *anything* you can to take the first step away from the table. Baby steps are easier to wrap our minds around than giant sweeping change. A little physical exercise can make you feel great about doing something healthy for your body and charge you full of endorphins, which are biochemical compounds that make us feel happy. Do something positive to get the endorphins flowing such as go for a walk or bike ride. In fact, one of best ways to get over someone is to get under someone else!

He-toxing can be like quitting smoking, full of stops and starts. But it gets easier, so don't give up on yourself! When I was he-toxing from Jack, spending time in Mexico with two of my closest friends reminded me of how much fun and carefree I was before we started dating. A couple of times when I was in my cups, I slipped and text paged him. But generally, my friends supported me and I filled my day with stuff I wanted to do and by the time I got back, I was feeling much better.

You may not have the time or money to go to Mexico for a week, but there is always something more fun to do than feeling like a miserable victim.

Chapter 12
F*ck Buddy Rules of Conduct

> *You cannot make yourself feel something you do not feel, but you can make yourself do right in spite of your feelings.*
>
> ~ *Pearl Buck*

Far too often, melodrama occurs when people engage in casual sex. Have you ever wondered why if there is a penis going willy-nilly in a given group of friends, you might as well put your shit slickers on because it is about to rain poo? Here are some guidelines to minimize the angst that can arise when sex is commonly happening outside of committed relationships.

1. Everyone should be on the same page. Make sure you both know the duration of the relationship up front. One night, one weekend, the course of one business convention, whenever you want to get a little and nothing better is available etc. Otherwise you can acquire a reputation for being a "Clingon," and in extreme cases, a "Stalker."

2. Be honest with yourself about what you want. If you are telling your f*ck-buddy that you really don't want a relationship outside of sex, don't expect them to treat you like a significant other. No long emails talking about your childhood and what you are like as a person. No daily calls to say, "Hi." And for the love of Pete, no getting pissed when they sleep with your friends.

3. Be polite. If you feel like chewing your arm off when you wake up... resist the urge to flee. For whatever reason, a fleeing f*ck-buddy inspires a little something called, "bruised ego." This condition, if gone unchecked, can lead to low self esteem and neurotic behavior. If you want the f*ck-buddy to be cool, YOU need to be cool.

4. Never call a f*ck-buddy fat behind his/her back. It will get back to them and really make you look like an asshole.

5. While it is ok to sleep with your f*ck-buddy's friends... it is NOT ok to screw them in your f*ck-buddy's bed. This is

what we like to call, "a f*ck-buddy-foul." Have some common sense!

6. On sleeping with your f*ck-buddy's friends. I personally love to get my (now ex) f*ck-buddies laid, but if you are one of those who feels territorial about yours do us all a favor and don't sleep with anyone... ever. Just because you kicked down some ass once or twice does not make you the King/Queen of that person's dating pool.

7. When your f*ck-buddy is starting to get attached and you can feel your self desperately wanting to flee, be honest and tell her she is making you feel cornered. If you start ignoring her calls and not answering her emails... she will start getting that icky feeling I described in #3 having to do with a bruised ego. And girls, remember NO CLINGONS, it makes the process tidier.

8. NEVER try to force a one-night stand or one-weekend stand into something it's not.

9. Be protective of your f*ck-buddy. I have very special relationships with every one of my ex-f*ck-buddies. I have spectacular taste in men, so they are all people I consider friends in one way or another.

10. Put the good vibe out there. You know everyone talks. You don't want to be an ass, everyone will know about it and you'll get a horrible reputation. If someone gets clingy, it's ok to STOP feeding the kitty and put in some distance, but do it nicely. And be honest. Tell her/him that you only wanted a one night stand, that she isn't "the one." And never make promises you don't plan to keep. It's just creepy. Don't talk about your family and how close you are, or the cute outfit your ex-girlfriend left at the house you want to give to her. I mean those are things that are telling her she might be "the one" and mixed signals are always a bad thing.

BE HONEST, BE CLEAR!

Chapter 13
The Man's Perspective

by Brion Porter

When I met Brion, he was a legendary ladies man (some would say "Ho") within my well traveled peer group. He is the archetype of the babe-magnet and an expert on dating like a man. I've asked him to speak on the subject of dating in general and how he met his perfect match (me, of course!).

From most people's perspective my girl and I met in a rather unusual way. In essence, we met with instant animal attraction. We both saw something we wanted and went for it. Within seconds we were making out (much to the dismay of our friends who had just introduced us), and within minutes we were in bed together.

I am not sure about Rachael, but that kind of know-exactly-what-we-want attraction was unprecedented for me.

What I didn't realize at the time was she would be unparalleled as a perfect partner for me. I knew right away that I wanted her, and that did not change as we had further opportunities to be with each other.

Some would ask, "How did you know she was perfect?" I know it is cliché, but I just felt it. Every part of me wanted to be with her. With that feeling I pursued her, and she seemingly welcomed it. That is a HUGE first step to a lasting relationship.

> ### Rachael's Thoughts
> This is typically what we think of as love at first sight. Some would call it lust at first sight and that would be equally as apt. Men seem to be very in touch with their carnal instincts. If he is going to be in love with you, he will very likely want to tear your clothes off the first chance he can. This doesn't always lead to love, but it is a good start.

All traditional BS aside, I have found that women want to be wooed. So if you want to be with her and you figure out the way in which she wants to be wooed, then you are on the right path. With the amazing amount of chemistry we had, we just felt most comfortable being with each other, almost night and day. We never tire of each other's presence.

Many other aspects of a relationship are needed, like trust and communication, common interests, similar goals in life, etc. But what really is at the core of it all is compatibility. Call it chemistry, call it fate, call it whatever you want. But when you fit together like my girl and I do, you better be ready for the long haul, because that is where you are headed.

Chapter 14
Give Guys a Break!

Treat a man as he is, he will remain so. Treat a man the way he can be and ought to be, and he will become as he can be and should be.

~Goethe

The prevalent man-bashing in the modern dating landscape is a load of crap. Men are more than capable of a high standard of ethical behavior. In fact, they want to be loved and respected as much as we do!

My friend Cory is an intimidating mountain of a man. Acerbic and self absorbed, he has a bit of a cad reputation. He knows I adore him and he secretly does small things for me just because. He isn't trying to get in my pants, he just wants to be loved and appreciated for who he is. Men like to impress us. Give them credit for being wonderful and fabulous too.

When my friend Laura's son enlisted in the military shortly after the horrific happenings of 9/11, we were anxious and worried by his dangerous new undertaking. I came to his going away party with a heavy heart; worried this lovely young man would soon be leaving for the most hazardous of endeavors. I found him talking to friends with his seven year old sister snuggled in his lap.

He looked so grown up in his uniform, but the impish child was still evident. He saw my hands shaking as I went to hug him and he flashed a teasing grin. He explained that he was doing what he could to protect me, his mom and his little sister from further horrors.

This beautiful boy-man was putting his life on the line to protect the women he loved from danger. I was overwhelmed with appreciation at his chivalrous sacrifice. In that moment he was our knight in shining armor.

The most offensive thing about a few of the dating books I read the summer of 2005 was their poor their treatment of the male of our species. Why would we even be bothering with them in the first place if they were heinous jerks? Let's show some respect for the amazing men we know by holding dear to our hearts what we love about them!

Nine Things I love About Men:

1. They wish we would make ourselves a top priority so we could stop being pissed off at them for being high maintenance. Focus more energy on our own happiness!

2. The way they look at us when they don't think we are looking.

3. No matter how oblivious we are of our addictive draw, or how maddening we might be, or how bad the PMS, they are still utterly captivated by us.

4. No matter how tough we are, they want to beat the shit out of things that hurt us.

5. They are fearless spider killers.

6. They possessa certain sweetness and vulnerability.

7. Men are in awe of our power and pull; they know we have their hearts in the palm of our little hands and they respect that!

8. Regardless of what common dogma is they really do want to find a nice girl who adores them and live happily ever after. Because men are cool like that.

9. Kissing — sadly, it's not done enough in my estimation.

Conclusion

*To free us from the expectations of others, to give
us back to ourselves – there lies the great, singu-
lar power of self-respect.*

~Joan Didion

Society rarely encourages women to ignore convention.
This isn't that book. Know your worth, look out for
Number One, trust your instincts and settle for nothing less
than spectacular.

I've been in good relationships and bad ones. I've lived
on my own and with others. Frankly, some of the best times
of my life were when I was single and not looking. Spending
time with my fabulous kids, my beloved girlfriends and
guyfriends and doing whatever I want with no significant
other expecting large chunks of my time, commandeering
the remote control, or wanting me to play mommy is an
extravagant luxury that every woman should experience for
at least one consecutive year of her life.

Women would serve themselves well to abandon the

mindset that we need to be in a relationship, we need to have kids before we are 40 and maybe the perfect guy isn't out there so we need to find a guy that is passable and make it work.

Who says you need these things? How are these "needs" producing happiness or meaning in your life? Wouldn't you rather focus on something you actually have some control over like your job, or being a good parent, or seeing Venice?

It's so Hard to Take Care of Ourselves Sometimes

When I was writing this book, my girlfriends, family and Brion were all cheering me on but the most common comment I heard was, "Some people are not self aware enough to do these things!"

This is total nonsense. Being a doormat isn't fun for anyone. Using past hurts and injuries as an excuse for poor choices makes it tough to feel like we are capable or worthy of extraordinary relationships. Being miserable is a self perpetuating endeavor.

Most of us fall for the wrong guy at least once in our lives.

I've fallen for many Mr. Wrongs. The difference is, what should we do when the relationship ceases to be healthy? Have a system and the tools to terminate it.

You may not always have control over how you feel, but you do have control over your actions and that will become self perpetuating too.

If you expect a high standard of behavior, and walk away when your standards are not met, you will be shocked by the dramatic change in how you feel about yourself. You are your Valkyrie, your protector. All of the glorious things women do for the world, you can do for yourself.

Protecting my feelings and mental health was my top priority during the break-up with Jack. I was sad that the relationship was not working as I was deeply in love with Jack. That said, I was still unwilling to sacrifice my standards to maintain the relationship.

I had to do something to remove myself from the situation and refocus on the positive things in my life. Robin has been my best friend since I was ten years old. We take regular trips to this little town in Baja called San Felipe. Even though I was tempted to sit around in my jammies moping after I broke up with Jack, I packed my bathing suit and stoically got on the road for the 14 hour drive to Baja.

By the time I crossed the border, I felt a hundred times lighter. As I pulled into the condominium complex and saw the pale salmon adobe walls, I felt Zen. When Robin padded over barefooted with a big smile on her face and an icy cold beer for me, I was almost light headed with relief.

San Felipe has a very shallow beach that goes out for about a hundred yards. At night the tide goes out revealing the ocean floor to the starlit heavens. We took flashlights and the kids and explored the alien world exposed to us, mud squishing up between our toes.

One night a tropical lightening storm raged over the ocean. We opened up the windows and wrapped ourselves in terry cloth robes and watched it ominously get closer. We marveled at the raw power of nature and the haunting fury of the storm.

During the day we melted in with the other tourists visiting the sleepy town in its off-season. Because the town is in the middle of a desert, most of the food is plucked right from the ocean with small gardens providing supplemental fruits and vegetables. Everything is only hours old and the food is amazing in its freshness and simplicity.

Robin and I frequently sat at the Bar Miramar and had a San Felipe Shrimp Cocktail. We talked about life and love and flirted with the cute bar tender, who spoke hardly a word of English. Robin patted my shoulder and told me to vent if I wanted to, but I was looking out the window at the pale blue ocean sprawled in front of me; I didn't really feel like it. Her husband sweetly bought me a cerveza and told me I was a fabulous cool chick.

All of my senses were engaged by this relaxing trip with people I love. It was exactly what I needed to refocus my energy. Doing something pleasurable for yourself when you are feeling down is a great way to put distance between yourself and a bad situation. If you don't take care of yourself, then who will?

There are so many loving and constructive things we can do for ourselves when we are feeling down. Make a fun list of the things that make you feel good and keep it close by. Make yourself a priority. You are worth it.

Develop a New Hobby!

Here are a few of the millions of hobbies and activities you can participate in, most have organized clubs you can join.

Hobbies that get your blood pumping:

- Ballet
- Basketball
- Belly Dancing
- Biking
- Golfing
- Hurling
- Ice Hockey
- Jazz dance
- Racquetball
- Rock Climbing
- Rollerblading
- Rugby

- Skiing (water and snow)

- Soccer

- Softball

- Surfing

- Tennis

- Volleyball

- Windsurfing

Hobbies that inspire through art:

- Calligraphy

- Candle Making

- Casting

- Jewelry Making

- Learn to play an instrument

- Pottery

- Puppetry

- Scrapbooking

- Sewing Victorian or Elizabethan dresses

- Water Color

- Woodworking

Hobbies for the mind:

- Astrology
- Astronomy
- Game Playing
- Genealogy
- Map Making
- Writing

Useful Hobbies:

- Beer Brewing
- Bread Baking
- Cheese Making
- Cooking
- Gardening
- Pastry Baking
- Wine Making

Sort of Odd Hobbies, but there are Yahoo groups glorifying them!

- Beach Combing
- Bell Ringing
- Bubble Blowing

- Dumpster Diving
- Kiting
- Lock Picking
- Tombstone Rubbing
- Treasure Hunting

Other Fun Stuff to Do:

- Archery
- Audition for a play
- Ballet
- Ballroom Dancing
- Birding
- Bungee Jumping
- Camping
- Cave Exploring
- Civil War Reenactment Camping
- Hunting
- Jazz Dancing
- Learn how to Hula or fire dance
- Learn how to play an instrument

- Medieval Camping
- Paragliding
- Salsa Dancing
- Skydiving
- Yoga

Make your own list:

1. _____

2. _____

3. _____

4. _____

5. _____

6. _____

7. _____

8. _____

9. _____

10. _____

Glossary

Glossary of terms:

(1) **F*ck Buddy**: A sexual partner outside a committed relationship. Being "just friends" and having sex relations.

(2) **Polyamorous**: The practice, or acceptance of having more than one intimate relationship at a time with the full knowledge and consent of everyone involved. Polyamorous perspectives differ from monogamous perspectives, in that they respect a partner's wish to have second or further meaningful relationships and to accommodate these along-side their existing relationships. (Wikipedia)

(3) **Stop feeding the kitty**: To stop having sex with a woman. It references the fact that if you feed a stray cat, it will never leave.

(4) **Myspace**: A fun and addictive web site where you can create a personal space for blogs, music etc.

(5) **Clingon**: An individual who does everything in their power to form a relationship, often leading to unwanted attention even after the individual is told that the recipient is not interested in the proposed relationship.

(6) **Double Bagging**: The act of using condoms in conjunction with another form of birth control such as the pill or an IUD.

Made in the USA
Lexington, KY
22 February 2011